Forty Footsteps

Copyright © Linda Marie 2021

All rights reserved.

This book, or parts thereof, may not be reproduced, stored in a retrieval system, or transmitted in any form or by any means, electronic, mechanical, photocopying, recording or otherwise, without the written permission of the author.

All scripture references are from **The Holy Bible, New International Version.**

ISBN: 9798487013200

Book Design by Mary Reynolds
Book Cover by Mary Reynolds
Photography by Linda Marie

lindamarie40footsteps@gmail.com

Available on Amazon.com

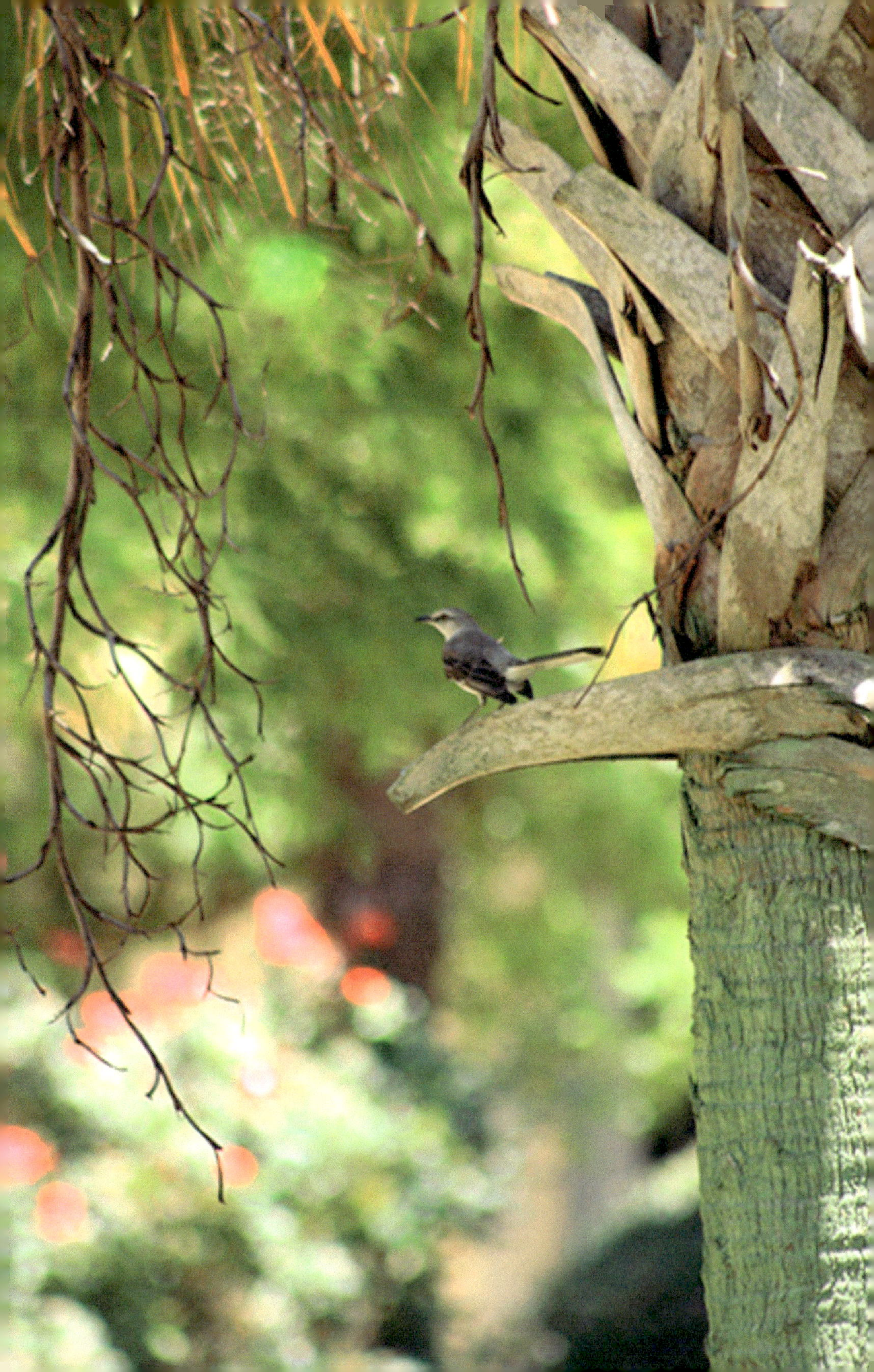

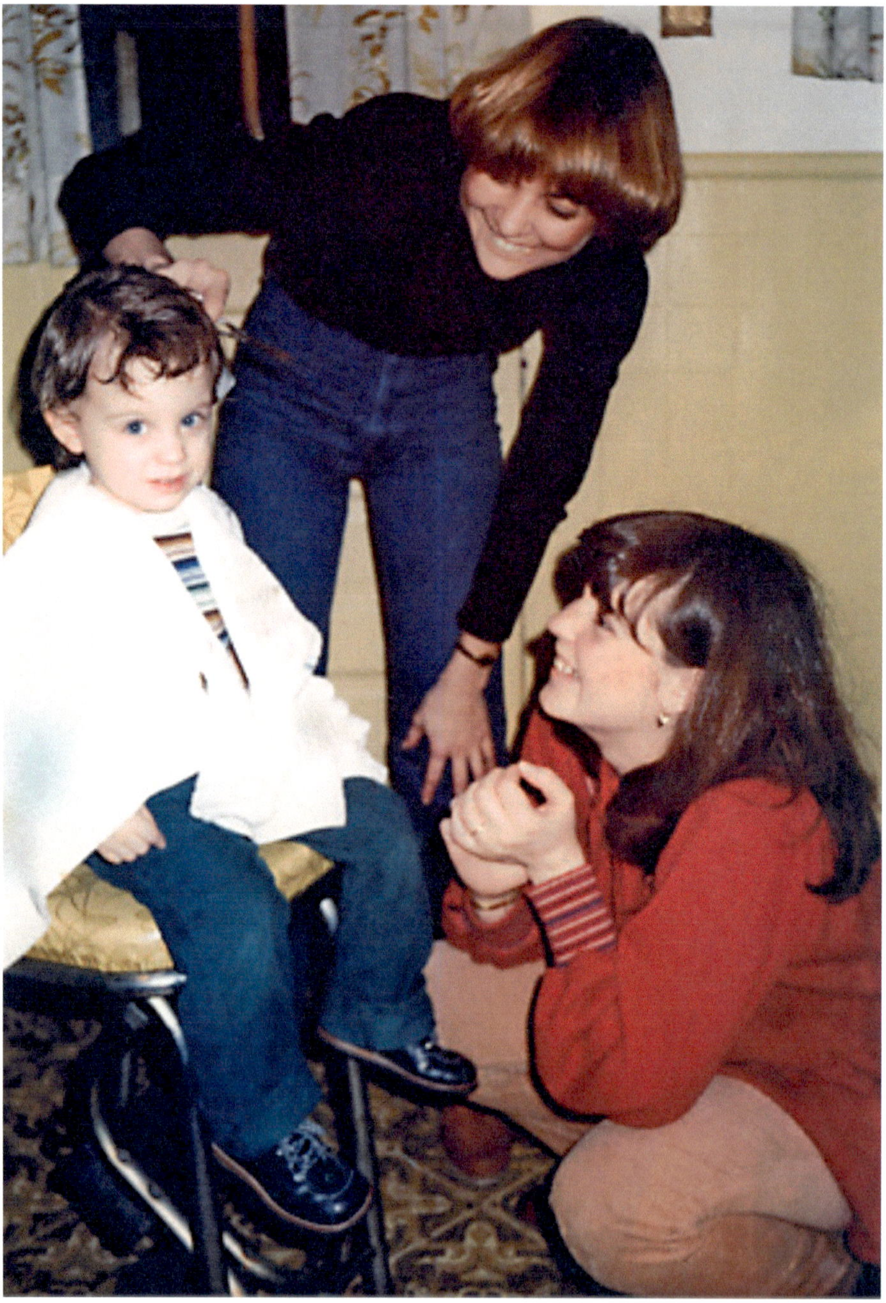

FORTY FOOTSTEPS

A HAIRSTYLIST'S WALK WITH GOD

LINDA MARIE

Table of Contents

Welcome..9

What You Will Need............................11

40 Day Devotional and 40 Day Prayer
    Journal..12

Closing Prayer Service 93

About the Author..................................96

Welcome

Forty is a significant number in the Bible. Moses and the Israelites wandered in the desert for forty years. Before Jesus began his public ministry, he was led into the desert to pray and fast for forty days and nights. In many Christian traditions the preparation time for Easter is remembered through a forty-day period of prayer and fasting called Lent.

Forty has also been a significant number in my personal life. It was at forty years old that I hit a particular time that can only be explained as a desert time. After rushing through life from one set of circumstances to another and finding myself tired and in need of replenishing, I prayed, slept, and began to pay attention to the little things, noticing the ways that God was trying to speak to me through my everyday experiences.

It is true that many times people tell their hairstylist things they tell no other person. The hair salon is a place of community. It is a place where the outer needs for beauty are addressed, and inner needs are revealed, where people gather to communicate their experiences of life. I have had the privilege to share in the hopes, dreams, and struggles of people from all walks of life. Forty Footsteps is a compilation of thoughts from over twenty-five years of such conversations.

It is only through faith in God, and time spent in his presence, that we are able to thrive and find peace in a world that is ever changing and challenging. Taking time to reflect on our daily experiences gives us a chance to regroup, and also to celebrate the good of God. In this way all things become occasions of prayer.

This book was created with the prayerful intention to encourage and facilitate a closer walk with God for the reader. I have included in this book a guided journal that has prompts to help, should you decide to write. Also included is an experiential prayer service to offer thanks to God for all the experiences of our lives; *for all things work together for the good for those who love the Lord and are called according to his purpose.* (Romans 8:28)

The devotions and journaling can be done for forty days in a row or at your own pace. They can be used as part of a Lenten practice or at any other time of the year. Done individually, or in a group, they can be quite rewarding. Thank you for choosing this book for a time of renewal.

What You Will Need

- An open heart and willing spirit
- A few minutes of quiet time to read the devotions
- Several minutes more to write in the companion journal
- A calendar to date your pages before you begin
- An ink pen

For the Final Prayer Service

- About an hour of time
- Some colored pieces of card stock paper
- A printer
- A pair of scissors
- A decorative glass jar
- Something to play music

Day 1

For years I worked in a salon with a woman who had a largely older clientele, and I was always struck by the kindness with which she treated her clients. The women had been coming for decades, many with appointments side by side. After so many years, they became friends. Although there was an individual nine, ten, and eleven o'clock appointment scheduled, three people would regularly show up at nine o'clock. This was their time to catch up with each other, to share stories of loved ones, to elicit prayers for hardships, to feel and to be connected to a community. As an observer, it was a lovely thing to see. Upon finishing each and every client the hairdresser would give them a pat on the shoulder and a warm hug. One day she told me she never forgets to hug them good-bye, because that may be the only hug they get all week long. This touched me profoundly.

As we move through a time of transition, due to the COVID-19 situation, we pray: Dear Lord, we thank you for the blessing of established relationships. Give to us the understanding of how to best help each other. Let our words be more loving, our hearing more attentive, and our service to one another more meaningful. Dear Lord, thank you for the simple opportunities to live the message of your great love.

John 13:34-35 A new commandment I give to you, that you love one another as I have loved you. By this all men shall know that you are my disciples.

Date _____

When have you had the opportunity to extend love to someone not in your immediate family? When have you had someone not in your immediate family extend love to you?

John 13:34-35 A new commandment I give to you, that you love one another as I have loved you. By this all men shall know that you are my disciples.

Day 2

    I drive in my car over the bridge joining the two sides of town, and there in front of me as I breach the top of the rise, is a panoramic view of magnificent proportions. Tall clouds, irregular clouds, filled with light, others filtering the light, billowy, wispy, literal castles in the sky.

    I don't know if I always noticed the clouds other than when I was a child. Children notice many of the important things in life, clouds, insects, puppies, kittens, and ice cream... I met a person once who said she came from a place that hardly had clouds. I remember being surprised by that. Ever since, I have taken special notice of the sky, and it is amazing that God would paint such beautiful pictures for us each day, ever changing, moment by moment, an upward canvas full of beauty just for the taking.

    We are so easily preoccupied with looking in front, behind, down, and just the lifting of our eyes can lift our mood. Lord, please help us to remember to look up, to seek the simple yet extravagant examples of your love and care.

Psalm 19:1 The heavens declare the glory of God; the skies proclaim the work of his hands.

Date _____

When was the last time you really took notice of the clouds in the sky? Describe what you saw and how it made you feel.

Psalm 19:1 The heavens declare the glory of God; the skies proclaim the work of his hands.

Day 3

I love the beach. It is my happy place. The smell of the salt water, the steady pounding of the surf, even the prickles from the sand, are a pleasure to me. I, who am not an athlete, can walk for hours at the beach.

It is like a treasure hunt. First looking out into the ocean, hoping to see a dolphin, then in the air, maybe a brown pelican will cruise by, but it is the shells on the shoreline that are the most captivating. I walk a little then stop and sift through the sand, so many shells to choose from, all colors and sizes, some broken some not. I can remember saying to God one day, "You know it would make me really happy if I looked down and found a perfect conch shell." Then less than a minute later, I looked down and there it was, the smallest yet most perfect conch I have ever seen. I had pictured in my mind a large shell, but my niece said, "God knew you would want to show it to everyone, so he gave you one small enough for your purse." When I look at this shell, I also think God wanted me to remember, he pays attention to the details. No request is too small to ask of him.

Dear Lord, we pray for trust. Let us not wait for the big things, but to come to you in prayer about every detail of our lives and person, for we know you care about it all.

Luke 12:7 Indeed, the very hairs of your head are all numbered. Don't be afraid.

Date _____

Where is the place that makes you feel happiest? Describe it and the way you feel there.

Luke 12:7 Indeed, the very hairs of your head are all numbered. Don't be afraid.

Day 4

This afternoon I got stuck in traffic. This gave me the opportunity to watch a young policeman standing in the middle of the eight-lane intersection direct traffic. This intersection locals sarcastically call "the Bermuda Triangle of Florida." I myself am anxious when stopping for a turn, in a two-thousand-pound car, at this highway. But this policeman wearing only his uniform and a bright green vest, with a whistle in his mouth and flailing hands, had it all under control. I wondered, "Do they take classes for this?" Honestly, once I let go of the time factor it was quite enjoyable, like watching some kind of strange choreographed dance between cars.

I thought about how many things, these men and women in uniform, do each day that go unnoticed or unappreciated. I know there are some bad police officers. There are some bad people in any profession, but I believe the majority of police officers are good. We thank you God for the people who strive for order and protection in our world, and for all first responders.

We pray, Heavenly Father please place a hedge of protection around these guardians of our safety and health. We pray also for their families who make many sacrifices. Guide them in all decisions and give them peace and joy.

John 15:13 Greater love has no one than this: to lay down one's life for one's friends.

Date _____

Write about your feelings toward the people who are in the police department or who are first responders, such as paramedics and firemen.

John 15:13 Greater love has no one than this: to lay down one's life for one's friends.

Linda Marie

Day 5

Today I turned down a breakfast invitation with friends, for the simple fact that it is the end of the month, and I really couldn't afford a meal out this week. This is new for me. I am trying to gain more control of my finances, and to show by responsibility my gratitude for God's blessings.

I am grateful for a place to live and a soft bed to sleep in, food in my stomach, so many things. When I see a person riding a bicycle down the street, I say a prayer. Some ride for exercise, but so many ride from necessity. There is such a stigma attached to poverty, and no one can convince me that all people who suffer financially have been irresponsible and reckless. This fact is never more evident than when looking further than our country, and out into the greater world.

Dear Lord, we pray for all who struggle financially. Please help us to not look at ourselves and others with judgment and condemnation. Help us to trust in your providence. Let our love for you be our motivation for change.

Matthew 6:28 See how the flowers of the field grow. They do not labor or spin.

Date _____

What are some of the advantages of living on a budget? Do you go to God in prayer about your finances?

Matthew 6:28 See how the flowers of the field grow. They do not labor or spin.

Linda Marie

Day 6

If God were holding this pen what do I think he would say. What he has said, has been written and spoken for millennia, and there is also private revelation, his voice within the heart. Today in my heart, Lord, I feel as if you are telling me "Relax my child. I have this covered." You say to me as you say to others, that all is filtered through your hands. For me, I know for certain, somehow, you know my innermost thoughts, and that only You could have fashioned the coincidences and synchronisms that have been such a huge part of my life.

Today we pray to be more open to your voice, to rest in the peaceful assurance that you love us and will guide us in the way that leads to joy and fulfillment.

Hebrews 10:16 This is the covenant I will make with them after that time says the Lord. I will place my laws in their hearts, and I will write them on their minds.

Date _____

What are some things you can do to free up more time to listen to God's voice?

Hebrews 10:16 This is the covenant I will make with them after that time says the Lord. I will place my laws in their hearts, and I will write them on their minds.

Linda Marie

Day 7

I stand under the silver canopy and feel the light sprinkle of warm water. Soon it is a torrential downpour of steaming rivulets hastily sliding into the shower drain. I reach for the bottle of green apple shampoo and close my eyes as the suds light as méringue and soft as a cloud, cleans my hair that is really never actually dirty. As I stand there rinsing the suds, washing my body, rinsing again, I think of how fortunate I truly am. So many people have no access to this luxury that I so easily take for granted each morning, and many will never have the experience of clean water in any setting, much less in such extravagant use. Dear Lord, help us to be always mindful of the generous blessings you give to us.

We thank you Father of all, for the water that cleanses the body and your living water that cleanses the soul.

Psalm 51:10   Create in me a pure heart, O God, and renew a steadfast spirit within me.

Date _____

What is something that you take for granted? Now that you have identified it, write about why you are thankful for it.

Psalm 51:10 *Create in me a pure heart, O God, and renew a steadfast spirit within me.*

Linda Marie

Day 8

Earlier this week while walking into a convenience store, I passed a young man in shorts, with blonde hair and a surfer's haircut. I immediately noticed his prosthetic titanium legs, and then hoped I didn't stare. I waited behind him in line. When it was his turn, a man edged in front of him. He could have said something, but he didn't. Instead he waited patiently. At his turn, he said in a calm voice, "You need to turn the pump on aisle ten." As he walked out, I noticed for a second time how smoothly he walked and wondered how long it took to master not just the walking, but all of it.

I thought about his soft voice and how so many times people mistake a soft voice, or an act of kindness or politeness, as weakness. This polite person with the soft voice had to be an incredibly strong person. In my mind, I said a prayer for all the people who struggle with any form of disability or differentness. I prayed for this young man, our young people coming back from war, and for those who have suffered catastrophic accidents.

Dear Lord on this day we pray that you watch over our young people and all who have physical challenges. Please give them the strength to remain kind in a world that at times is anything but kind.

Matthew 5:3-12 The Beatitudes Emphasis on
Blessed are the pure in heart, for they will see God.

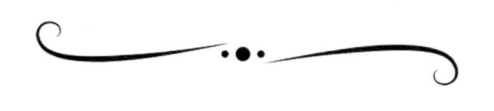

Date _____

What does it mean to be pure in heart? How can we nurture ourselves and others?

Matthew 5:3-12 The Beatitudes Emphasis on
Blessed are the pure in heart, for they will see God.

Linda Marie

Day 9

It is a glorious day. The sun is shining. The air has just a hint of cold, which is great for us Southerners who have been praying for cooler weather, but didn't really mean it! I have gone to a park that is full of different gardens, and they are spectacular. However, I know the names of very few different trees or flowers.

There are beds of pansies and tulips. The pansies are like tiny little faces smiling in bright and happy color. Tulips in red and yellow stand tall and reach for the sun. Roses of many different styles. I do recognize roses. They bring back happy memories of my grandfather who loved to fish and used fish heads, eggshells, and coffee grounds, to fertilize his beautiful beds of roses and tomato plants.

There are so many trees with leaves of gold, green, burgundy and orange. I recognize the Live Oak trees with roots so massive and deep. I remember climbing them as a child and hiding in their nooks, watching the world below.

Dear Lord, you have placed so much beauty around us and such variety. Help us to remember that there is beauty not only in the variety of nature, but in people of all shapes and colors, all origins and domiciles.

1 Corinthians 15:41 The sun has one kind of splendor, the moon another; and star differs from star in splendor.

Date _____

What is a characteristic that you have that is unique? How can you use this to the glory of God?

1 Corinthians 15:41 The sun has one kind of splendor, the moon another; and star differs from star to star in splendor.

Linda Marie

Day 10

I saw the movie *Bohemian Rhapsody* and cried and cried afterwards. It is hard to pinpoint one reason for so many tears. I know I thought of a close friend from high school who later went to beauty school, and at a young age died of AIDS. He was so talented and so fun to be around. I went to his senior prom with him. We went to the same beauty school, and it was then that I went to a drag show for the first time. He was not a drag queen, but a guy from school that we were both friends with was. I went with a group of students, some gay some not, to the Q, a local bar. The first night I saw our mutual friend perform as Dionne Warwick.

The friend performing, like several students, was on a list for surgery. I remember how surprised I was by it all. It was fun but there was also to me an undercurrent of sadness. I was eighteen years old and went home and wrote a note to God in my journal: "Thank you God, for giving me a body I can live with.

Oh, sure I'm not thrilled with the extra curves that I've acquired here and there, or the fact that my figure may never be anything to brag about, but it is a body that is female, a fact I delight in. I cannot imagine what it is like to have all the feelings of a gender you can never possess, but I think it must involve a lot of suffering."

Philippians 2:12 Continue to work out your own salvation with fear and trembling,

Date _____

Think of one thing you like about yourself and one thing you struggle with.

Philippians 2:12 Continue to work out your own salvation with fear and trembling,

Day 11

One of the hardest parts of my job is the waiting. I have to wait thirty minutes for a color to take, wait fifteen for a perm, wait only two minutes at the register for a card transaction to go through. Yet, even those two minutes can feel like eternity to me. There is a book about love languages. For some their love language is tangible gifts. For others their love language is words of encouragement or gifts of service. Whatever your love language, this is the thing that makes you feel loved by another. A friend of mine jokingly said she thinks God's love language is for us to wait, or waiting, and I think she is onto something.

So many times, I make a prayer and want an immediate answer or response. Sometimes I get it, but usually I have to wait. I don't wait easily for anything, but I have found if I do wait, if I don't rush in and try to fix things myself, if I give God the time, he comes through. Many times a problem that originally seemed like a mountain is easily remedied. It makes sense, if even a simple hair color comes out brassy or, in other words *wrong* if taken off too soon, then there is a certain timing in the right solution for the right problem.

Dear Lord, help us to grow in patience and trust in you. We pray for ourselves and those who are waiting or will wait, that you will give them the confident assurance of your presence and care.

Isaiah 40:31 But they who wait on the Lord shall renew their strength.

Date _____

What is something that you were happy you waited for?

Isaiah 40:31 But they who wait on the Lord shall renew their strength.

Day 12

According to Wikipedia, the logo of the little girl with the umbrella in the rain, and motto of Morton Salt, "When it rains it pours" was created when the company began adding magnesium carbonate to make their salt free-flowing even in rainy weather. Before researching this, I was thinking because of the age of the ad that it may have some religious connotations. Also, because for some reason when I looked at it while cooking, I thought about the Bible verse we are to be the salt of the world, and the fact that in life when it rains it usually pours. I looked at that logo with the little girl and the umbrella and thought of how we are to become like little children relying on God, and thought what is our umbrella when it begins to rain? After some consideration, I would have to say that prayer, scripture, fellowship, and childlike reliance on God are given as gifts to be mine and others' umbrella when the rain comes. This keeps our lives from becoming flat, and allows us to give flavor to the world.

Please Lord, give us the desire to come to you regularly in prayer and obedience, noticing all the wonders and instruction you give to us moment by moment. We thank you because when the rains do come, we have the umbrella of your love to keep our gifts free flowing.

Matthew 5: 13 You are the salt of the earth. But if the salt loses its saltiness, how can it be made salty again?

Date _____

What are some things that you do that make you feel closer to God?

Matthew 5: 13 You are the salt of the earth. But if the salt loses its saltiness, how can it be made salty again?

Linda Marie

Day 13

I have an anonymous quote on my wall that says, "Those who want to sing will find a song." The truth of it called to me at first glance. It was at a time in my life where nothing seemed to be going right, and yet I had this overwhelming urge to sing. I found myself waking up at least an hour early each morning, so I could listen and sing to a variety of music before starting my day. I was conscious of God's presence and of sharing this time with him. I listened to songs from Gladys Knight like, "If Anyone Should Ever Write my Life Story" to "God Will Make a Way Where There Seems to be no Way" in tandem with each other. Though it took quite a while for my outward circumstances to change, inwardly there was comfort immediately.

I heard a talk about a tribal tradition where when someone experienced a great loss, this person would go to a place alone and sing for thirty days as their grieving process. I have also heard that those who sing once pray twice. This all sounds wonderful to me, and I have experienced the benefits.

Dear Lord, we ask that you help us each to wake and keep a song in our hearts throughout the day. Please let us offer those moments of pleasure and joy for our healing and the healing of the world.

Psalm 71:23   My lips will shout with joy when I sing praise to you- I whom you have delivered.

Date _____

What is your favorite song? Do you feel you sing or praise God enough?

Psalm 71:23   My lips will shout with joy when I sing praise to you- I whom you have delivered.

Linda Marie

Day 14

Last year, waking to the news of another horrific tragedy, my first thought was that this may not be the big end of the world, but this end is just as final for many, and those who survive will bear the scars forever. I prayed.

A few days later I was invited to a concert by Craig Morgan. My friend had won great tickets, very close to the stage. Craig Morgan is a master storyteller and has written many songs. This was his American Stories tour and the revenue was used to benefit a national non-profit organization that he partnered with to provide mortgage-free homes to veterans. After singing a couple of songs, they set up five chairs and microphones. Three other singers were seated along with Clint Romesha, a recipient of the Medal of Honor and author of the book *The Red Platoon*. Then for the next two hours they went around the circle sharing stories and songs. The music was excellent and the stories inspiring. We live in a wonderful, yet heartbreakingly broken, world.

In the Gospel, John speaks of Christ, and we are reminded that "The light shined out in the darkness and the darkness couldn't overcome it." (John 1:5)

We are to be Christ for the world. Our world is in great need of an outpouring of random acts of kindness, songs of praise and gentle melody, prayer and helping hands...

It's time to let our light shine.

Date _____

When you hear let your light shine, what does that mean to you? What do you feel is your light?

John 1:5 The light shined out in the darkness and the darkness couldn't overcome it

Linda Marie

Day 15

I drive in my car today and watch the sun dance across my windshield. It is cold outside, and the extra warmth from the light feels good. I am on my way home from a special presentation by some military people on Veteran's Day. I am so thankful for life in a free country. I heard some interesting information. One surprising fact was that only one percent of the population in our country has direct experience with the military. This creates a gap in community understanding.

Used to be a person served a tour and then was back home, but now our military men and women are serving, coming home, and then going out over and over again. This greatly increases the incidence of PTSD. It is so difficult to go through the actual experience of war, the killing, the destruction, even just the noise and chaos of it all. Then to come back to a country and circumstance that is so vastly different, sometimes creates a void and a loneliness for the person who has lived on the edge and is now trying to adjust to a "normal routine."

Dear God, thank you for the brave men and women who serve our country. Please be with them and their families. Please open our eyes and fill our hearts with gratitude. Please heal the scars of war and guide all men and women towards peace.

Luke 9:24 For whoever wants to save their life will lose it, but whoever loses their life for me will save it.

Date _____

What causes you to have a sense of patriotism? What causes you to feel thankful for our country?

Luke 9:24 For whoever wants to save their life will lose it, but whoever loses their life for me will save it.

Linda Marie

Day 16

Those who fail to remember the past miss out on experience's greatest gifts. Mistakes and things considered failures, though unpleasant to remember, are often life's most valuable teachers. Nostalgia, fond memories, they serve a higher purpose than normally recognized. These memories provide not only comfort and healing warmth, but also help us to document some of life's most daring ventures. Just think of those first flights at Kittyhawk, or the first polio vaccine, or the first time a person looked at a computer screen and had access to the information highway…

God has a plan for each of us here. Even at the very end, we may never know if our special part in the Plan was present in our defeats or victories. Therefore, we endeavor to run the race well, as Paul instructed in the Bible, not for the perishable wreath of this life but for the imperishable.

We thank you, Lord, for the gift of perseverance and ask that you remain by our sides guiding us through all of life's twists and turns.

Philippians 1:6 being confident of this, that he who has begun a good work in you will carry it on until completion until the day of Christ Jesus.

Date _____

What is one thing you would consider a victory and one a defeat for you?

Philippians 1:6 being confident of this, that he who has begun a good work in you will carry it on until completion until the day of Christ Jesus.

Linda Marie

Day 17

If we wish to build a better world, or have any desire to live with some semblance of peace we must remain open to change. We must continue to try to understand ourselves and remember who is the keeper of our heart. Otherwise, we will never find the answers to the questions: "Am I my brother's keeper?" or "Who is my brother?" Those who have eyes to see, or are not afraid to look, witness what happens when an individual or society gives up the struggle. A great sadness and emptiness appear. We see it in records of suicides, poverty, murder, wars…that continue in horrific headlines in countless newspapers.

To give into the comforts acquired in this life, or to the despair created by a lack of comfort, guarantees these questions will never be answered. Our world is in desperate need of some authentic hope, and this hope can only come from a base of mature love.

Heavenly Father, you love us with a love that is totally unconditional, a love that we as humans can only touch upon, through the grace of your spirit. Yet you gave us an explanation, of the love we should pray to extend to each other. Please help us to see the intrinsic beauty in every person and to respond with love and grace towards each other.

Corinthians Chapter 13 The love chapter: Love is patient. Love is kind…Love never fails…These three remain faith, hope and love but the greatest is love…

Date _____

Do you resist change? When was a time when you made a change out of love for another person?

Corinthians Chapter 13 The love chapter: Love is patient. Love is kind...Love never fails...These three remain faith, hope and love but the greatest is love...

Day 18

When I was in my late twenties, I met and became friends with a remarkable lady who was eighty years old. She had bright blue eyes, soft silver hair and the figure and energy of someone half her age. Her friendship with my family became sealed when my mom was visiting and flooded the kitchen while doing laundry. She ran next door, and soon she and Edna Mae were racing into the house, mops and buckets in hand. Together they got up all the water before I got home, and my mom relished in the telling of how my eighty-year-old neighbor had saved the day.

I learned a lot from Edna Mae. She was a strong woman of faith. We shared many life experiences together, some pure delight, some of deeper life lessons. Edna Mae talked in detail about the loss of one of her teenage sons. After his death, she went through her days in solitary silence. It was the darkest time of her life. Only one morning, months later, when she heard herself humming, did she know she could and would go on.

Dear Lord, we pray for the mothers, for all the moments of joy and for all the moments of pain that come in some form or another to all mothers. We give thanks to the blessing that each carry by bringing new life to the community and world.

Luke 1:38 "I am the handmaid of the Lord," Mary answered. "May your word to me be fulfilled." Then the angel left her.

Date _____

What is a loss that you have experienced? How did God help you to make it through?

Luke 1:38 "I am the handmaid of the Lord," Mary answered. "May your word to me be fulfilled." Then the angel left her.

Linda Marie

Day 19

Though many times a mystery, one certainty in life prevails. Things will come and go, and alter each new moment. Our body, our first and lasting companion throughout life will surely change. All physical structures do. And the country of our youth, will either thoughtfully or carelessly submit itself to change. By the time the next generation reaches the age of reason, even in such a short span of time, the country of our birth may be unrecognizable to us.

Therefore, there is no tangible unchanging place called home, and the intangible home of the heart will either grow into mature love or atrophy. Unlike a physical structure, the home of the heart is not contingent on any superficial feature or event. A perfect example of this thought in action, is when we look at the inspired quote of Stephen Hawking, "Where there is life there is hope." Where there is life there is hope, Lord, and we as Christians have the added hope and assurance of the resurrection of the earthly body and the receiving of a glorified body in heaven. Help us to be mindful of the great gift of the body, and to respect and care for it appropriately. Whatever its form or shape, we thank you for this great blessing.

1 Corinthians 6:19 Do you not know that your bodies are temples of the Holy Spirit, who is in you, whom you have received from God?

Date _____

What is one thing that you can do to improve your physical health?

1 Corinthians 6:19 Do you not know that your bodies are temples of the Holy Spirit, who is in you, whom you have received from God?

Day 20

No one can remember their first vision of this world. Was the hospital top notch, but was the first light harsh and the room cold. Or was the room dimly lit? Did you by chance arrive plunging into a pool of tepid water? Were you immediately cuddled in a soft warm blanket, then held to your mother's full breast? Or did you arrive in a sweltering room, and then placed on a hard dirt floor? Did anyone hold or comfort you when you cried? Did you arrive in perfect health? Did you have all your vital parts? Was your system free of drugs or other poisons? On that first day, did you writhe in pain or slumber in comfort?

Babies who are loved and cared for are healthier. That is true of both physical and emotional health. They begin with an inner confidence that comes from an early history of having their needs met, along with being valued as a precious gift.

Dear Lord, we pray for those who do not have a loving person to tell their story, or to walk with them in love from beginning to end. We pray for all to know the wonder of your great love. We ask to be made mindful of the iniquities of life and to work for change.

Psalm 27:10 Though my mother or father forsake me, the Lord will receive me.

Date _____

What is your favorite birth story? It can be your own, someone else's, from the Bible, from a spiritual experience...

Psalm 27:10 Though my mother or father forsake me, the Lord will receive me.

Linda Marie 51

Day 21

Babies will grow into toddlers, to children, to teens, and then adults. Genes, and first families, give important details; yet they are only doorways to a larger world. Questions are keys for each new passage. Remembering the house and vistas of our childhood is like looking through a kaleidoscope. Depending on how you turn the dial, the perspective, the picture, changes shape and size. The memories that are burned into our psyche, or fixated by choice, create a picture that may be factual, but at the same time may not be truthful.

There is so much to be said about perspective. Three siblings can grow up a few years apart, and yet when sharing memories, it can seem that they must have lived in separate houses. Also, no matter how wonderful or troubling, remembrances are not active life any more. They are only memories. Each must be seen as part of a continuum. So many families and relationships fall apart because of memories, and others are shored up, made firm, by common happy memories.

Dear Lord, help us to learn from the unhappy memories and treasure the good. Help us to keep the perspective that this life is fleeting and love is of highest value.

John 13:34 "A new command I give you: Love one another as I have loved you, so you must love one another."

Date _____

What is one of your favorite childhood memories?

John 13:34 "A new command I give you: Love one another as I have loved you, so you must love one another."

Day 22

I walk into the grocery store with aisle after aisle of great food items. All of the cans, boxes and bags are aligned in pristine order. All are placed for easiest convenience and to entice. Then there are the vegetables and fruits, bright red apples, orange oranges, crisp green lettuce...all the colors of the rainbow represented in produce. Now most grocery stores even have flowers for sale. How fortunate am I to live in this day and age and country!

I feel sometimes being in the grocery store is as uplifting as being in a beautiful building or lush scene in nature. I thank you, Lord, for the abundance of blessings you open up to so many of us. Even if I die tonight with my small bank account, I have lived like a king compared to so much of the world. Let us not be greedy with the blessings we receive in all forms both material and spiritual, and with an open heart full of gratitude, let us give what we can give to make this place we inhabit truly heaven on earth.

Psalm 27:13 *I remain confident of this: I will see the goodness of the Lord in the land of the living.*

Date _____

What is your favorite food? Have you ever experienced true physical hunger?

Psalm 27:13   I remain confident of this: I will see the goodness of the Lord in the land of the living.

Day 23

Soon I will take a warm shower, dress in nice clean clothes, and drive my car to a job I actually love; yet, sometimes I wake up sad for no reason at all. It has taken most of a lifetime to learn that I can choose what I decide to think about. I can take the time to sort out where the sadness originates, or I can shift my thinking to something pleasant.

This morning I choose the latter. I think of the lineup of people who will sit in my chair today, and I am thankful for the opportunity to serve them. It is amazing how a little snip with the scissors here and a splash of hair color there can brighten someone else's day and, in the process, brighten mine. Lord, help me to be thankful for the gift of good honest work, for the ability to support myself in a respectable manner.

Dear Lord, please bless all those who search for work, and those who work in jobs of service.

Colossians 3:23 Whatever you do, work at it with all your heart, as working for the Lord, not human masters.

Date _____

What is the work that you feel God has given you in this life? How does it feel when you put your whole heart into this work?

Colossians 3:23 Whatever you do, work at it with all your heart, as working for the Lord, not human masters.

Linda Marie

Day 24

Far too many people get barely a glance in this life, and there are those whose lives begin and end before their fifth birthdays. Studies have shown, when a baby's basic needs such as food and shelter are not met, many will suffer from the "failure to thrive syndrome." Additional needs like eye contact from a loving person, interested chatter, gentle touch, physical and mental stimulation must be acknowledged as vital at any age.

The effects of care present at birth will continue to show up later in life. Sometimes, although the beginning is strong, certain life events can leave a person bankrupt of that initial cushion. A significant lack at any point in life can impact one's perception, abilities, and realized goals. I am reminded of a television program I watched that personalizes this assertion. As an articulate homeless man was being interviewed, he looked down at the floor and said, "The hardest part of being homeless is being invisible. No one makes eye contact with me anymore."

Dear Lord, help us to regard all people with the dignity that you have made an indelible part of being human. Let us push past our discomfort to help another.

Genesis 1:27 So God created man in his own image, in the image of God he created him, male and female he created them.

Date _____

Talk about a time that you were able to help another person with no thought of reward.

Genesis 1:27 So God created man in his own image, in the image of God he created him, male and female he created them.

Day 25

Oftentimes when I am driving, I am struck by a particular tree or plant that seems to jump out and scream "I am wonder and light!" Usually it will be a very special tree stuck between two ordinary looking ones. It is always something about the way the light catches the leaves that causes it to shimmer in the sunlight. This morning I noticed a Maple tree flanked by two evergreens.

The leaves of the Maple were golden and orange, and seeing it for only an instant as I drove by, made me again appreciate the everyday treasures that God surrounds us with. The way the sun hit the leaves made some shine like silver dollars, metallic in the light. Up against the Maple, the green from the other trees looked almost lime in color. Simple, really simple, and like I said for only a moment, but if we train ourselves to look, then life is full of small and deceptively simple delights.

Dear Lord, open our eyes to the wonder of your ways.

Proverbs 2:1-5 My son if you accept my words and store up my commands within you, turning your ear to wisdom and applying your heart to understanding—indeed, if you call out for insight and cry aloud for understanding, and if you search for it as for hidden treasure, then you will understand the fear of the Lord and find the knowledge of God.

Date _____

What is a hidden treasure that you have discovered in life?

Proverbs 2:1-5 My son if you accept my words and store up my commands within you, turning your ear to wisdom and applying your heart to understanding—indeed, if you call out for insight and cry aloud for understanding, and if you search for it as for hidden treasure, then you will understand the fear of the Lord and find the knowledge of God.

Day 26

To err is human, to forgive divine. That saying has always resonated with me. When I think about it, I see why some sayings are passed down and have meaning generation after generation. It is because the words speak to an inescapable truth.

Sometimes I err in everyday little ways, by maybe saying something carelessly or in a hurry, and then realizing that I have accidentally hurt someone's feelings. No matter how small the infraction, I am so relieved when the other person gives me some grace and forgives the offense.

I grew up with a person who was not given much grace in her childhood. She erred and she was not forgiven. As an adult she was able to forgive big and small offenses in a distant relationship, but not able to forgive those close to her.

I have found that the root of much unforgiveness is fear. The fear that if I forgive, I will be hurt again. The fear that when I need forgiveness, it will not be given and, again, I will be hurt.

Dear Lord, please give us the courage to ask and grant forgiveness, for it is only through your divine presence and love that this is possible. Please help us to learn to apply forgiveness as a healing balm in all our relationships.

1 John 4:18 Perfect love casts out fear.

Date _____

Is there something or someone you need to forgive? Write about a time that you benefitted by forgiving or being forgiven.

1 John 4:18 Perfect love casts out fear.

Day 27

It is after dark when I get home tonight and it is very cold and rainy. I think to myself, "Why does it always seem it has to rain before it gets cold here?" As I walk up the driveway, the cold and wet coming up from the road feels like tiny glass shards. I remember a recent conversation where I was complaining of the cold and someone at the table said, "Oh, I am so happy we are getting some cold weather. The colder the better. It will kill off a lot of the mosquito and insect larvae for the summer."

I can't help but wonder how many times things that seem annoying and unnecessary in everyday life may be paving the road to an easier or more beneficial time later. We are not in heaven yet, and so everything cannot be smooth sailing. Actually, if it was, I don't think we would know how to handle that in this lifetime. The fall of Adam and Eve is a permanent part of our history, and God is so gracious and so loving that he immediately put into place a plan of redemptive value, that includes the suffering and trials we go through in this life. He has promised to work all things out to the good for his children.

Dear Lord, please build our trust in you, to know you are working for our good even when we can't see it.

Romans 8:28 And we know that in all things God works for the good of those who love him, who have been called according to his purpose.

Date _____

Can you remember a time that you suffered and later felt that you benefitted from the experience? Could you see that God brought something good out of the pain?

Romans 8:28 And we know that in all things God works for the good of those who love him, who have been called according to his purpose.

Day 28

I sit in a group feeling not quite in sync with the other members. I hear things I don't agree with, or a thought that I think could use clarification. Sometimes, I just want to share things I am excited at having learned or have begun to understand. I try to keep my mouth shut, but before I know it I am interjecting. Later I know I will worry that I talked too much, and question if my assertions were right.

I think all people, especially Christians, go through a certain amount of this. The key is, is it true? Is it kind? Is it necessary to say? First of all, we have to be sure what we speak is true. This means do we have firsthand knowledge of what we speak. Secondly, is it kind? Some very unkind things are spread around under the guise of asking for prayer. Would we want this particular thing discussed if it were about us? Could we not just ask another person to pray without giving details? Is it necessary? The Bible says we will give an accounting of all unnecessary words. There are so many good and true things to discuss. Please, Lord, move our conversations in that life-giving direction.

Dear Lord, please guard our mouth and give us discernment in the things we say. Give us a sincere desire to hear and understand another's thoughts.

John 17:16 They are not of the world, even as I am not of it.

Date _____

When was a time that you said just the right thing at just the right time? When was a time when you were at a loss for words and relied on prayer?

John 17:16   They are not of the world, even as I am not of it.

Day 29

There are few greater pleasures than to spend time with friends and loved ones. The banter between two close friends can rival any tennis match in excitement and mental exercise. The hug of a child or caress of a loved one can outperform any massage in relaxation. The simple pleasure of sitting in the presence of someone you love, and who you know loves you, is a gift sometimes too rare, and always pure delight. We thank you Lord for those you have put in our lives to love and who love us in return. The very first thing you said that was not good in the Bible was when you said it is not good for man to be alone. In this age of high technology, it is so easy to become caught up in meaningless activity and to sacrifice the one-on-one or group relationships you created us for.

Yet, there is also a gift in this technology, especially when meeting in person may not be advisable or possible. We turn our thoughts towards the blessing of technology and ask that you guide us in using it to build up one another spiritually, relationally, and physically.

Please help us to be mindful of one another, to make time for each other in the best possible form.

Proverbs 27:17 *As iron sharpens iron, so one person sharpens another.*

Date _____

Who is your closest friend? What do you love about them?

Proverbs 27:17 As iron sharpens iron, so one person sharpens another.

Day 30

When I go to God in prayer, I know that he is really here with me, and all those empty places inside of me are suddenly made full. I can search and search and will never find a human being that can fill all those spaces, and this expectation that another can guarantee happiness is a burden too great for any one human.

How amazing that we are granted access to the creator of the universe by simply opening our hearts and calling on the name of Jesus. I look in wonder at the surroundings he has created for us, the birth of a newborn child, the opening of a flower, the flight of a bird... our thoughts, our memories, the things we feel and see and touch...and I am humbled by such great love.

Dear Lord, you have given us blessings in abundance. Please help us to never forget that you are the true source of our joy. Help us to love one another and enjoy all you have given, while keeping you at the center of our lives. And when we cannot feel you, help us to turn to your Word, to turn to you in prayer, with assurance that you are and will always be with us.

John 1:1 In the beginning was the Word and the Word was with God, and the Word was God.

Date _____

Write about a time when you opened up the Bible and knew that God was speaking through His Word.

John 1:1 In the beginning was the Word and the Word was with God, and the Word was God.

Linda Marie

Day 31

The ancient Hebrews regarded a name as a prized possession. A name not only identified a person but a name was also a way of knowing a person. To have no name was to have no value. Jesus has many names, Wonder Counselor, Prince of Peace, Christ…yet Jesus is above all other names. We likewise have many names, wife, mother, father, son, daughter…yet Child of God or Christian is our most valued name.

What does this name mean for us? Some of what it means is that the power of the name Jesus is available to us at all times. We are also children of a God who is so loving that we can barely realize the breadth and height of that great love. He sent his Son to us and when Jesus returned to heaven, he sent His Spirit, the Holy Spirit, leaving us with the fruits of the Spirit: kindness, gentleness, love, peace, self-control, joy, faithfulness, goodness, and patience.

Dear Lord, when we are identified, named as a Christian, please give us the grace to lead lives that reflect our knowing the creator of the universe, the Father, Son and Holy Spirit. Let others come to know His name through our witness, love and example.

1 John 3:1 Behold, how great a love the Father has lavished on us, that we should be called Children of God!

Date _____

Jesus asked Peter once, Who do you say that I am?" Who is Jesus to you?

1 John 3:1 Behold, how great a love the Father has lavished on us, that we should be called Children of God!

Linda Marie

Day 32

On the way to church services, I was ruminating about a person who had hurt my feelings. I knew I needed to forgive that person and most assuredly should not have been thinking about the offense on the way to church. As I was driving, out of the corner of my eye, I saw a man who I guessed was homeless on the side of the road, and I noticed he was leaning over the grass. What caught my attention is that I could clearly see his index finger pointed towards the ground. I looked in my rear-view mirror to make sure I had seen what I thought I had. There he was with one hand in the grass doing who knows what, maybe looking for something. When I originally noticed his index finger, I was instantly reminded of when Jesus leaned over and wrote something in the dirt. Jesus's final message was: "Let he that is without sin cast the first stone."

I finished my drive thinking that if I want other people to understand when I make a mistake and forgive me, I need to be willing to do the same for them.

Dear Lord, help us to let the little slights that happen go by. Help us to realize that they are all really little when you get down to it. You sent Your Son to forgive All our sins giving us the ability to love and forgive each other freely. Help each of us to grow in forgiveness.

Luke 11: The Lord's Prayer "Forgive us our trespasses as we forgive others..."

Date _____

Is there someone you need to forgive? Write a prayer for this person.

Luke 11: The Lord's Prayer "Forgive us our trespasses as we forgive others…"

Linda Marie 75

Day 33

I sit in my chair looking at a poster of a painting, *The Goldfish*, by Matisse. It is my favorite. It has in the background lavender, green, pink and yellow foliage, and is of a gold fish bowl sitting on a wrought iron Louisiana style table. This painting was done years and years before Louisiana was the tourist center that it is today, and before a certain type of architecture or furniture would bring to mind a particular place like the French Quarter. And yet, here I sit admiring this picture which visually blends the old with the new. It is a mystery how art can transcend time, and life is full of mysteries.

Not all things are explainable. A major mystery is how God can be one and yet three, Father, Son and Holy Spirit. How could Jesus be true God and true man? Some things are true from physical facts, like the evidence of the resurrection. Some we accept on the basis of a relationship.

Dear Lord, please give us the strength to trust in faith the deepest mysteries of your presence. In a world where we are called to make decisions, where some or many of the facts may be mysteries, let us go to You in prayer knowing that Nothing is a mystery to You.

Job 42:2 "I know that you can do all things, and that no purpose of yours [Lord} can be thwarted."

Date _____

What is something you can pray for faith or discernment about?

Job 42:2 "I know that you can do all things, and that no purpose of yours [Lord} can be thwarted."

Linda Marie

Day 34

Recently I talked to a friend, Sam, who is one of the most interesting people I know. He is eighty-five years old, and I met him about thirty years ago. Then, he was just beginning to win the battle against a cancer that he was told would kill him in three weeks. He has been cancer free for all of thirty years, and he and his wife as a ministry, have helped countless others fight that battle. They have weathered the storms of adversity and been generous in times of prosperity. The best piece of advice that I have been given came from Sam. He said God will never ask you to do something wrong to achieve something right. Sounds simple, but when you think about it, not really. Multiple opportunities come up to use this sound direction.

He and his wife have been married for over sixty years. Many people who are married that long have similar temperaments, but Sam and Anne are the exception. She loves to read and the quiet. He thrives on activity and conversation which is great for me. Anne is happy to let us talk on the phone indefinitely. After all these years, they not only have a deep and abiding love for each other, but they really like and enjoy each other. They attribute all of their resiliency and joy to their relationship with God.

Lord, let us pray in thanksgiving and for protection for all the married couples who are bright lights in a dark world.

Ecclesiastes 4:12 A chord of three strands is not quickly broken.

Date _____

What is the most important facet of a beautiful relationship?

Ecclesiastes 4:12 A chord of three strands is not quickly broken.

Linda Marie

Day 35

I went to Catholic school for the first two years of education. It was long enough to learn to pray The Lord's Prayer; receive first Holy Communion; and learn from the Sisters about Mary, the Blessed Mother of God. Going into this Easter season I am thinking of the scene in the movie *The Passion* where it shows Mary's face as she witnesses the scourging of her Son. The Blessed Mother is the one who can understand all form of suffering, and yet who knows the glory of the promises of God. She was at Pentecost and was one of the first evangelists.

On a more personal note, I can remember spending the summer with my grandmother. I slept in the bedroom where she had old pictures of the saints on the walls, which were kind of scary looking. I was already afraid of the dark to begin with, and I would burrow under the covers. It is then that I would pray to God, and think of Mary as a loving mother figure.

Dear Lord, thank you for those early teachings of respect and love for the Mother of God.

Luke 2:34-36 Then Simeon blessed them and said to Mary, "This child [Jesus] is destined to cause the falling and rising of many in Israel, and to be a sign that will be spoken against, so that the thoughts of many hearts will be revealed. And a sword will pierce your own soul too."

Date _____

Who do you call on when you need prayer?

Luke 2:34-36 Then Simeon blessed them and said to Mary, "This child [Jesus] is destined to cause the falling and rising of many in Israel, and to be a sign that will be spoken against, so that the thoughts of many hearts will be revealed. And a sword will pierce your own soul too."

Linda Marie

Day 36

Sometimes the hardest part about being still is that we do have time to think... I know, for myself, that the recent news of the COVID 19 virus has caused me, at times, to do anything rather than be still. I have wanted to resume my hurried lifestyle, and to continue to strive towards immediate goals. I have wanted to feel some sense of accomplishment, rather than feel the uncertainty of this time.

Right from the beginning, though, God has been beckoning me as he has so many others, to be still and to know that He is God. To be still and alone is frightening. Knowing that God will never leave us or forsake us assures us that we are never alone. In His Word, He says over and over, "Do not be afraid for I am with you."

Dear Lord, give us the courage to use this time of unexpected stillness to draw closer to you. Teach us to hear your voice in the open spaces of our hearts, and lead us in the way that you would have us to go. You are all knowing and all loving. We pray for all who are suffering from this pandemic and place all in Your loving care.

Psalm 46:10 "Be still and know that I am God;"

Date _____

What are some things that you can do to make your living area more inviting for prayer and stillness?

Psalm 46:10 "Be still and know that I am God;"

Linda Marie

Day 37

Excerpt from Guadium et Spes
Pastor Constitution on the Church in the Modern World
Vatican Council II

Preface

"The joys and hopes, the grief and anguish of the people of our time, especially those who are poor or afflicted, are the joys and hopes, the grief and anguish of the followers of Christ as well. Nothing that is genuinely human fails to find an echo in their hearts."

This is a quote from a Church Council held in the sixties. The first time I read these words, I was struck by their beauty and the spirit of intent in them. Now, so many years later, we are realizing in our time, through this present crisis just how connected we are with each other, all around the world. So many people are suffering in so many ways, yet there is hope in the indomitable spirit of a people that turn their face to God.

Dear Lord, please give us the courage, stamina, and love, to live this time in our history, in the best possible way. Give us a heart for You and for each other. Give us the vision of the mystery of Your resurrection and the hope of a bright tomorrow.

Psalm 30:5 Weeping may stay for the night, but joy comes in the morning.

Date _____

What things do you feel you have in common with other people around the world? What challenges do all humans face?

Psalm 30:5 Weeping may stay for the night, but joy comes in the morning.

Day 38

I met my niece at a park last week. There was no hugging as we took our seats across from each other at a wooden picnic table. We each had brought sodas and snacks, and I pulled out the Scrabble game. We both laughed and chattered away as we put on disposable gloves to wear while playing. I am so very thankful that we have this time together. That she is willing to go to such lengths to play a game, and spend the afternoon with her aunt. It was so much fun, but oh how very odd life is nowadays?

She is young, and I am older, much older actually. That is one thing that this COVID-19 virus has done. It has made people very aware of ages. I hear some people complain that the younger people are not taking this thing seriously enough, and I think, "How can they really?" I still remember that feeling of being indestructible, and I love to see the sparkle in my niece's eyes when she talks about her recent marriage and the excitement of starting a family one day.

Dear Lord, so many people, young and old, are making sacrifices to help one another in so many different ways. Please help us all, both young and old, to keep meaningful connections. Loneliness and depression are not just a possible affliction of the elderly. Please keep us steady in our faith in you and fill our hearts with your joy.

Nehemiah 8:10 The joy of the Lord is our strength.

Date _____

Is there a family member or close friend that brings you joy?

Nehemiah 8:10 The joy of the Lord is our strength.

Day 39

I was sitting outside today and thinking how grateful I am for so many different things. I was daydreaming as I thanked God. The breeze was blowing. I was sitting in a rocking chair that faced the pool taking in the beautiful landscaping around the water. A few feet in front of me was an unattractive plant that looked like a small pile of hay, and there was a wasp flying around it.

I thought about how lately I have seen so many orange butterflies. I know this sounds weird, but even when I am driving there will be one flying towards my car. I was thinking, "I wish I would see an orange butterfly," when I saw another wasp. I thought, "I guess sometimes what you get is wasps." Then, right then, a small orange butterfly landed on that green plant, and I hurried to get my camera. It flew off the plant before I could get the picture, but it flew around my face several times before it was gone. I read up to see what an orange butterfly symbolizes, and it symbolizes that joy will come your way. I guess it's true. For that moment, I just knew God was listening, and my heart was filled with simple joy.

Dear Lord, thank you for the simple pleasures of life. Give us eyes to see and hearts that revel in these little surprises.

Job 12:10 In his hand is the life of every creature and the breadth of all mankind.

Date _____

Think of a time when God surprised you with some type of outward sign that He is here.

Job 12:10 In his hand is the life of every creature and the breadth of all mankind.

Linda Marie 89

Day 40

One of my favorite quotes is from a book, or series of books, called *City of God,* written by St. Augustine. This is what he says: "I have already said something of the general blessings of God, which in the natural course of things, come to the good and bad alike. However, beyond this bounty, He has reserved for the good a special sign of His great love. We can never sufficiently thank Him for the gifts of nature: that we exist and are alive, that we can enjoy the sight of earth and sky, that we have a reasoning mind that we can seek Him who has made all these things. Yet for the greater gifts of grace there are not hearts or tongues enough in all the world to ever try and thank Him. For when we were burdened and broken by our sins, and our eyes were turned from His light and blinded by the love of the darkness of iniquity, He did not leave us to ourselves, but sent to us his Word, who is His only son, so that, by His birth and passion in the flesh He assumed for our salvation, we might learn how highly God esteemed our human nature, and that we might be cleansed from all our sins by His Unique Sacrifice and, by His Spirit have Love poured into our hearts, so that, with all our warring over we might come to everlasting rest in the supreme blessedness of gazing on his face."

Hebrews 12:2 And let us run with perseverance the race marked out for us, fixing our eyes on Jesus, the pioneer and perfecter of our faith.

Date _____

Fill the page with blessings for which you are thankful to God.

Hebrews 12:2 And let us run with perseverance the race marked out for us, fixing our eyes on Jesus, the pioneer and perfecter of our faith.

Linda Marie

92 Forty Footsteps

Prayer Service

Take a moment to relax in the presence of God. Breathe in. Breathe out. Breathe in peace. Breathe out worry. (Pause for a few minutes.) We begin with a short and simple prayer.

- *We love you Father, Son, and Holy Spirit. We thank you for the many blessings you have given. Thank you for the time of this study and the new revelations that you have brought to mind. Thank you for the gift of life. Thank you especially for your love and acceptance of us and the promise that you will never leave or forsake us.*

Let your mind wander a little. Think of all the good things you've learned over these past forty days. Think for a moment of some things both good and bad that you are ready to leave as memories as you embrace a new and bright tomorrow. Sometimes it is just as important to leave behind some good experiences as it is to leave the difficult. This way our hands will be open to God's new blessings. (Pause for a few minutes.)

Take some time to write these thoughts down on the colored card stock, or print from your computer. If you are doing this with other people, take a few minutes to go around the room and let each share some of those memories .

Linda Marie

Play some music. Some suggested songs are:

- "God Will Make a Way" by Dan Moen
- "Lord I Offer My Life to You" by Heavenly Voices
- "My Wish" by Rascal Flatts
- "If Anyone Should Ever Write My Life Story" by Gladys Knight
- "Here I Am Lord" by Dan Shutte
- "I Say Yes/ Digo Si" by Donna Peña

Any song that makes you feel uplifted and close to God is good. A great daily habit is to sing for ten or fifteen minutes each morning before starting the day. It is said, "Those who sing pray twice."

As the music is playing take time to cut the memories on the colored card stock that you have either hand written or printed on a computer into small little pieces like confetti to be placed in your decorative glass jar.

Both the good and the bad experiences make us who we are. God promises to turn all things to good for those who love the Lord and are called according to his purpose. (Romans 8:28) Also, He that has begun a good work in you will continue it to completion until the day of Christ Jesus. (Philippians 1:6) (Take a few minutes to admire your handiwork.)

This glass jar filled with brightly colored paper is a reminder of the beauty and art that you have partnered with God to make in your life. As you go forward from day to day, you can take time to add to this jar. One day you will have a piece of art that is overflowing with lessons of God's love.

In closing we pray:

• Dear Lord, thank you for allowing this special time with You. We pray for our world, our country our leaders. Please help us to always be aware of your presence and loving care in our life, and help us to pass this love onto all others we meet. We love you Father, Son and Holy Spirit! Amen

About the Author

    Linda Marie has always had a great love for people, and for writing. As a hairstylist, she works with outer beauty, while listening to the hopes, dreams, struggles and greatest concerns, of many people from all walks of life. As a writer she puts these thoughts together. In **Forty Footsteps**, she shares her greatest love, God. This is a way of imparting hope in a world that at times seems to be spinning out of control, yet at the same time is full of beauty. She is a Stephen Minister, has a Certificate of Spiritual Direction and Theology, and was inducted into the Honor Society for Religion and Theology. She is author of a series of three children's stories with a character named Cleo the Cloud (*Cleo Goes to Rio, Cleo Goes Ballooning, Cleo's Family Tree.*) All three stories are available in one delightful edition called **The Adventures of Cleo the Cloud** on Amazon.com.

Notes

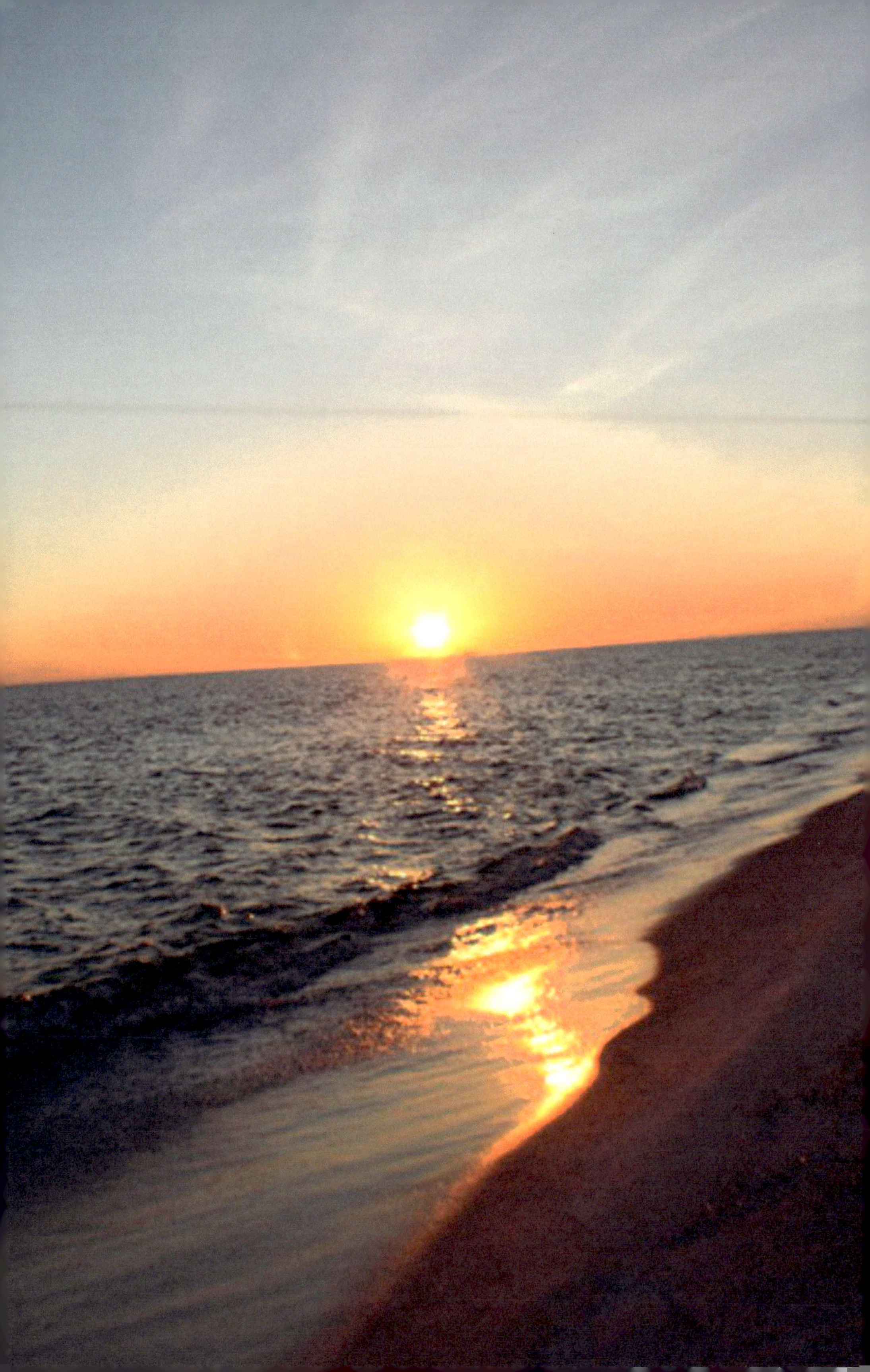

Made in the USA
Columbia, SC
30 August 2024